Woof!

ISBN: 978-1-68022-578-5

If Dogs Could Talk

new seasons®

No, because if I "drop it" you're just going to throw it again.

I'm only waiting tables until I get
a callback from Animal Planet,
which should be any day now.

Wanna go outside? Let's go outside. Can we go outside? We should go outside. Have you been outside?

I don't care how much they paid for the couch. I slept on the old one and I'm sleeping on this one.

I have to walk
her twice a day.

My backside smiles so much,
my mouth doesn't have to.

I'll hide out
here until
they put the
two-year-old
to bed.

I may not be able to run anymore, but I'm wise enough to appreciate the days when I could.

I know I messed up, but people really need to realize they can't have nice things <u>and</u> a puppy.

Mrs. Johnson owns us all, so yeah, I guess that means we're related.

They always say they'll
only be a minute.

I like the idea of a sandwich;
I just never have the patience
to actually make one.

Really? A sweater?
It's 100 degrees outside, lady.

We have to go home now.
I need to call my broker.

I ran. I got the ball.
I brought it back.
Now what?

I wasn't worried, until
he started calling me
his little meatball.

Yeah, I ate the boy's homework. That's what I love to do, eat boys' homework.

No squirrel may pass.
I am the Squirrel Master.

Uh, you guys might want to sleep downstairs tonight.

If I stand still and think
only happy thoughts, this bath
will be over in no time:
toilet water, squeaky toys,
table scraps...

Drop it. Drop it. Drop it.
Drop it. Come on, drop it.

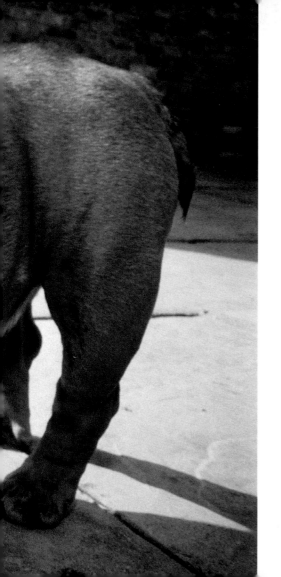

You're definitely
picking the wrong
day to mess with me.

There'd better be a prize at
the bottom of all this!

This is torture.

Someone call the authorities.

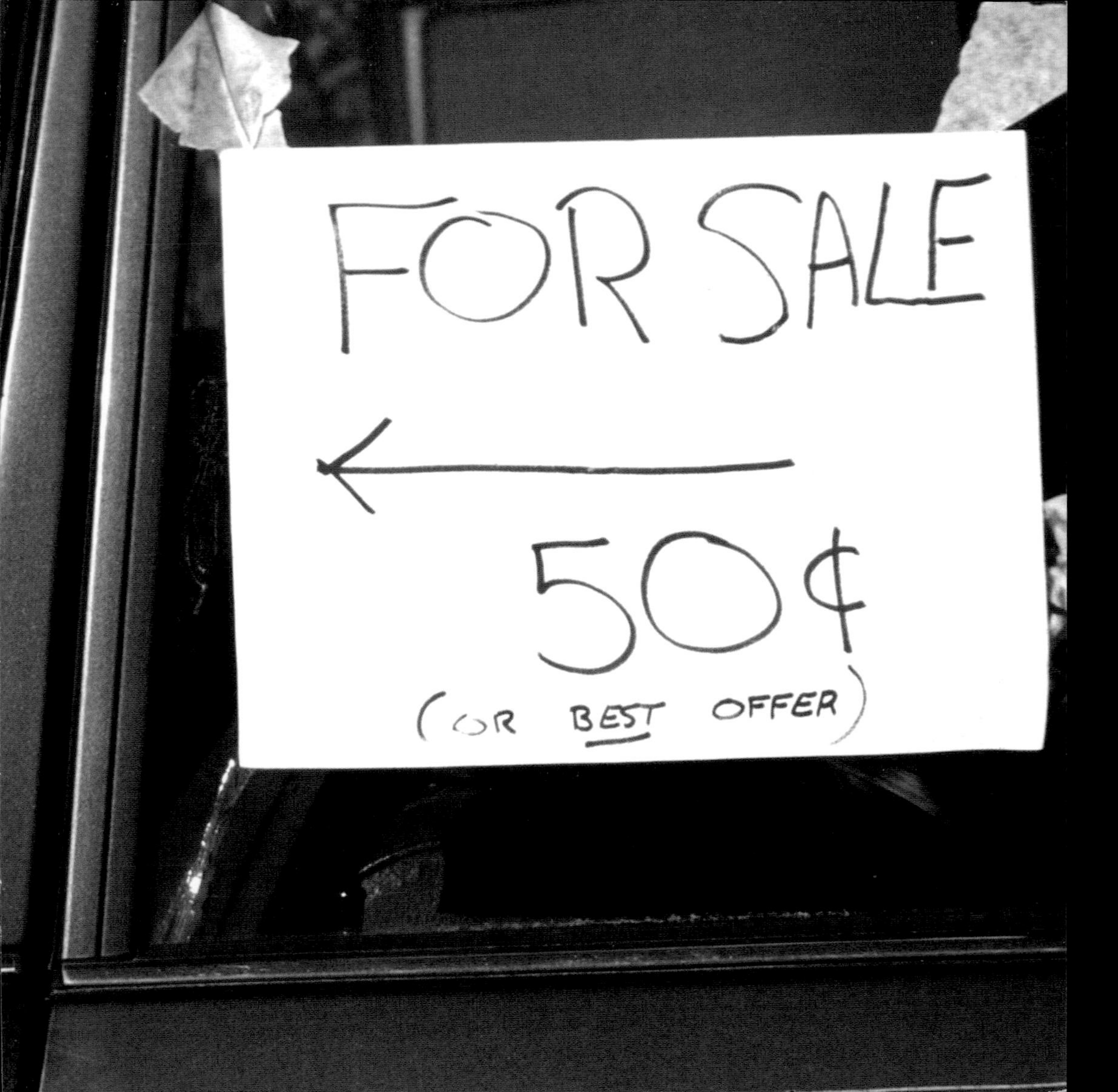
FOR SALE
←
50¢
(OR BEST OFFER)

Come on now, big girls don't cry.

Sometimes I feel I'm a
Jack Russell trapped in a
bulldog's body. But then
that goes away and I just
sleep the rest of the day.

What obedience class? I was trained on the streets.

Is that a box of tissues
left unattended?
JACKPOT!

What's she
laughing
about?

Man, did I fall asleep
in the wrong place...

I'll just bury the car
keys right here to
keep them safe.

Maybe if I chew this up enough they'll get rid of it.

Nobody knows the
trouble I've been.

Would it help if I said I'm sorry?

Delicious!

I <u>hate</u> going for walks,
but without me, the ladies
just <u>ignore</u> him.

Can you really blame me
for biting the groomer?

I plead the Fifth.

I thought you said these
were Jimmy Chews.

Are you in a "time-out"?

I just wanted to come with you.

Let's get outta here
before they realize we
raided their picnic basket!

Psst...

The humans are watching.

Do I smell ham?

When was there ham?

Everybody else is
sitting at the table....

We put the "pup"
in pup tent.

I'll take the blame if you
don't want to make the bed.

Be on the lookout for
the nearest fire hydrant.

I am the epitome of
the phrase dog tired.

I wasn't lost, you were.

The end.

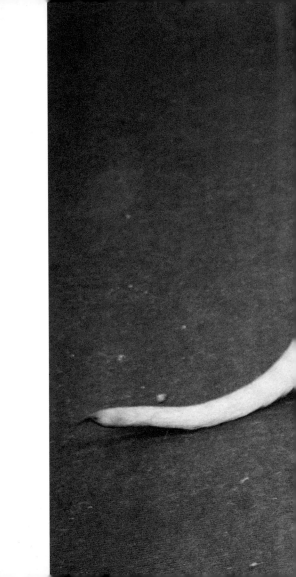